D0792339

STAR WARS

THE CLONE WARS

WHAT IS A
SITH
WARRIOR?

WRITTEN BY
GLENN DAKIN

CONTENTS

TIMELINE

The Clone Wars take place in a time between 22 BBY and 19 BBY (BBY stands for Before the Battle of Yavin). More information about this period is still coming to light, but the timeline shows some of the important events in the Clone Wars known to date.

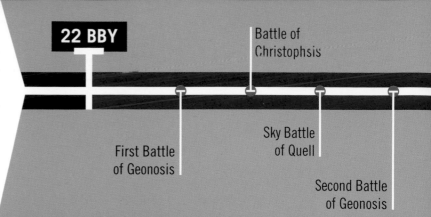

22 BBY

First Battle of Geonosis

Battle of Christophsis

Sky Battle of Quell

Second Battle of Geonosis

WHAT ARE THE CLONE WARS?

For centuries, the Sith have plotted the defeat of the Jedi, an ancient order of knights who are masters of the Force. By destroying their age-old enemies, the Sith could bring about a new era dominated by the dark side of the Force.

Now, Darth Sidious, the Sith leader, has started a war in the galaxy in order to bring his evil plan to fruition. Sidious's apprentice, Count Dooku, leads the Separatist forces as many worlds seek to break the rule of the Republic, led by Chancellor Palpatine and supported by the Jedi. The Separatists' vast armies are made up of battle droids, often led by the fearsome cyborg General Grievous. The Republic has mustered its own great army, a force of identical clone troopers.

The Clone Wars are spreading chaos across the galaxy, bringing it to the brink of darkness . . .

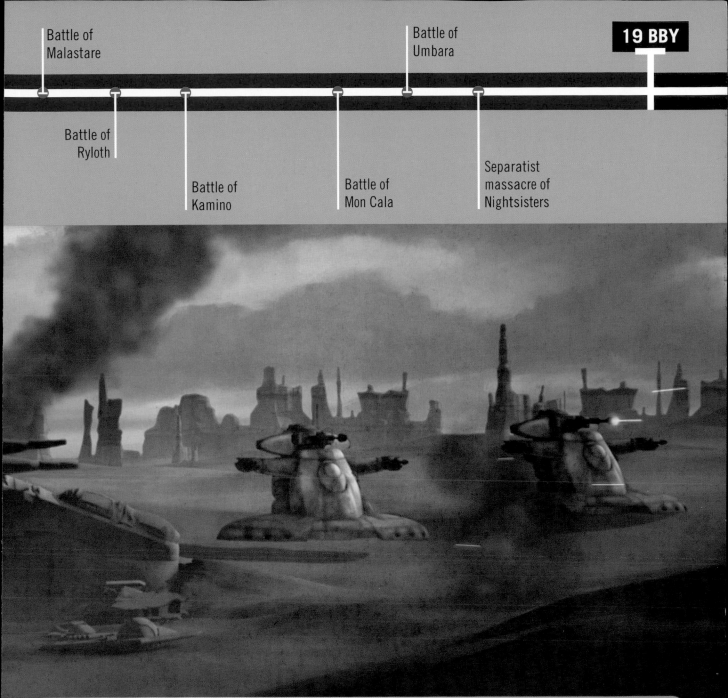

Battle of Malastare				Battle of Umbara		**19 BBY**

Battle of Ryloth

Battle of Kamino

Battle of Mon Cala

Separatist massacre of Nightsisters

WHAT IS A CLONE TROOPER?

Clone troopers are bred with a built-in sense of duty. They become fully grown, fully trained soldiers for the Republic's Grand Army in just 10 years. Each clone trooper is an exact copy of Jango Fett, a military expert and ace bounty hunter who helped set up the cloning program.

WHAT IS A SITH

Sith warriors are figures of mystery and menace, lurking in the shadows until it is time to strike. Masters of various forms of combat, Sith warriors show their foes no mercy. They believe that one day they will rule the whole cosmos and bring a new age of darkness.

SECRET WARRIOR

Savage Opress is a brutal Sith assassin who follows the orders of Count Dooku. Dissatisfied with his role as a Sith apprentice, Dooku believes he could challenge the might of their leader, Sith Lord Darth Sidious, and make Savage his own apprentice one day.

AMBITIOUS APPRENTICE

A Sith Master seeks to solidify their own rule and crush any foe who gets in their way. To do this they must take on a apprentice that will learn their skills and one day take their place. Sith apprentice Count Dooku has sworn to help destroy the Jedi and will take any chance to end their power, often in a terrible duel to the death. But Dooku is also compelled by his own burning ambitions.

WARRIOR ?

RULE OF TWO

Once, there were many Sith, but they fought amongst each other. The Rule of Two was brought in stating there must only be one Sith Master and one apprentice. But some Sith break this rule by training warriors in secret, hoping to take them as an apprentice one day.

FALLEN WARRIOR

Darth Maul was once Darth Sidious's apprentice. Defeated by Obi-Wan Kenobi before the Clone Wars, he was believed to be dead, and Sidious took on a new apprentice—Count Dooku. Now Maul is back and seeking revenge on the Jedi, yet cast out by his own kind.

HOW CAN THE LIGHT SIDE BE USED AGAINST THE SITH?

The dark side of the Force is powerful and seductive and gives the Sith an edge over their enemies. But there is another power, opposite to the darkness, which helps bring balance to the galaxy. The light side of the Force supports kindness, friendship, and peace—all things that the Sith do not respect. For the Jedi, the light side is a very powerful defense against the vengeful Sith.

SUPPORT

Key elements of the light side are law and order, and this is respected by the Republic. As a result, its leader, Chancellor Palpatine, supports the Jedi in all they do, providing them with armies of clone troopers, fleets of battleships, and powerful weapons. This massive military strength makes the Jedi a formidable enemy indeed.

WISDOM

The light side of the Force attracts the wise. Skilled Jedi, like Yoda, have managed to master the Force to such an extent that nearly no one can match their powers. While the Sith seek forbidden knowledge, which they guard jealously, the Jedi seek to share their knowledge. This wins them respect and valuable alliances.

LOYALTY

The Sith are united by their dedication to the dark side of the Force. They work together because they will be punished for failure. Friendship proves stronger than bonds created by fear. When a Jedi Master trains a faithful Padawan, a sense of teamwork is established that is powerful and rarely lets them down.

WHAT MAKES DARTH SIDIOUS A POWERFUL SITH LORD?

Darth Sidious is the mysterious leader of the Sith. Driven by a hunger for power, he is following an age-old plan to bring about the downfall of the peaceful Republic and the Jedi who guard it. Sidious's true identity is a secret and the Jedi do not realize the threat that he poses.

BLACK, HOODED
CLOAK HIDES
IDENTITY

TRUE OR FALSE?

Sidious hates the Republic more than anything.

False: His real hatred is for the Jedi.

WHO IS DARTH SIDIOUS?

Darth Sidious is a human male with dark powers that he is able to hide from the Jedi. He leads a double life and keeps his Sith identity a secret. The Sith Rule of Two allows Sidious only one apprentice at a time—first Darth Maul, then Count Dooku.

He Holds Great Power

Sidious has cleverly formed alliances with vast galactic corporations and powerful people. He knows he can call in favors from organizations like the Techno Union at any time, mobilizing their massive fleets of battleships and droid armies to bully or crush his foes.

He Is Ruthless

Darth Sidious is ruthless in destroying anyone he sees as a threat to his rule. When Count Dooku forms a team with Asajj Ventress, the duo are so successful that Sidious fears they might one day overthrow him. He coldly orders Dooku to destroy Ventress.

He Plans Ahead

Always with an eye to the future, Sidious constantly looks for new ways to entice Jedi children to the dark side. However, his plans rarely bring him success—Jedi protect their future Padawans very well.

WHO ARE THE ALLIES OF COUNT DOOKU?

To rule the galaxy, the Sith need more than just a mastery of the Force. They need armies, equipment, and resources. To obtain these things, they make alliances with key ruthless and greedy groups: the ambitious Techno Union, the scheming Trade Federation, and the warlike Geonosians.

The Techno Union

This mighty alliance of high-tech companies is led by Wat Tambor. The Clone Wars have created business opportunities on a massive scale for the Techno Union, and it has given its entire army of droids over to the Separatist war effort. Building ever more terrible weapons of war, they conspire with the Sith to plunge even the remotest parts of the galaxy into battle.

Weapons Of War

Much of the Sith's firepower and equipment is provided by the Trade Federation. Weapons, such as vulture droids, tirelessly seek and destroy Republic fighters using laser cannons and energy torpedoes. Their knowledge of space lanes, including secret hyperspace routes, also gives the Sith an advantage in the war.

The Trade Federation

Cold, calculating Neimoidians run this mega corporation, which has grown rich on the profits of war. The head of the Trade Federation, Nute Gunray, has put its droid armies at the service of the Separatists. In return, the Sith sometimes tell him which planets are ripe for plunder, and the Federation's forces move in.

Poggle The Lesser

Ruler of Geonosis, Poggle the Lesser controls the droid factories that make his world a powerful player in the galaxy. To help the Separatists gain victory, Poggle's scientists have created the B2 super battle droid as well as new super tanks. Count Dooku has promised Poggle that once the war is won, Geonosis will be a key part of the Confederacy of Independent Systems.

WHAT IS COUNT DOOKU'S SECRET WEAPON?

A master of combat, Count Dooku presents many threats to an enemy, yet there is one power he holds back. It can torment a foe and cause a painful death, but it also drains energy from its wielder. Only in a very dark hour does Dooku call forth Force lightning.

JEDI REPELLENT

The Jedi do not use Force lightning, as it is for attack and torture. They use the Force only for self-defense. Faced with its searing power, a skilled Jedi can absorb and deflect it, turning the lightning against its user. Anakin, however, has not yet learned to use this skill, which gives Dooku the edge he needs to defeat him! Force lightning can be deflected safely only by a true Master of the Force. Yoda can do it, but until Anakin Skywalker learns how to defend himself against it, he will never be able to defeat his Sith foe.

THE LAST RESORT

When Dooku uses Force lightning, masses of energy surges through his limbs, zapping his strength. However, after a fierce lightsaber duel against Asajj Ventress, Count Dooku realizes he has no choice but to call on this devastating power to drive Ventress back and escape.

CRUEL TRAINING

Force lightning may have a dangerous effect on his body, but Dooku considers that a small matter when compared to its effectiveness in training new Sith assassins. He blasts them with bolts of Force lightning to increase their endurance levels.

She Is A Nightsister

Ventress was born among the Nightsisters of Dathomir—sorcerers who know many dark arts for achieving victory in battle. Their magic has rubbed off on Ventress, and the witches support her in whatever she does, making Ventress a powerful ally.

**TWIN CURVED
LIGHTSABERS
CAN JOIN
AT THE HILT**

WOULD VENTRESS MAKE A GOOD SITH APPRENTICE?

To ensure that the evil reign of the Sith continues for all time, a Sith Master chooses a student of the dark side to one day take their place. This is known as the Rule of Two. Count Dooku has trained Ventress in the ways of the dark side, but not as a true Sith apprentice. Would she be suited to the role?

WHO IS VENTRESS?

Asajj Ventress is Count Dooku's most trusted commander in war and his most skilled assassin. She seems to be almost unstoppable. Even the Sith Lord Darth Sidious begins to fear her strength, and wonders if Ventress is perhaps too good a candidate for the role of apprentice . . .

She Was Force-Trained

... she was saved ... by Ky Narec. Seeing her potential as a powerful warrior, Ky taught her about ... combat and how to become one with the ... control her mind and feelings.

She Is A Loyal Follower

After the death of her Jedi guardian Ky Narec, Ventress made her enemy, the Jedi, her ... influence of the dark side of the Force and eagerly agreed to work for Count Dooku. Ventress became Dooku's formidable ...

WHAT IS IT LIKE TO BE LOCKED UP WITH COUNT DOOKU?

DOOKU, COUNT
1.93 M (6.4 FT)

As leader of the Separatists, Sith Lord Count Dooku is a bitter enemy of the Jedi. He could never imagine siding with them under any circumstances. But when Dooku, Obi-Wan, and Anakin are imprisoned by pirates, they are forced to share a cell and a common goal—escape!

HELPING HANDS

Dooku will take any help he can get, even if it is from his enemies. Bound together by their pirate captors, Sith and Jedi are for once able to talk together without exchanging blows. The cool Count stands separately and wonders whether the Jedi will figure a way out of their tricky situation.

FORCE POWERS

Dooku is a master of the Force, and he shows off his great skills from inside their prison cell. He lifts a plate of food with the power of his mind and brings over a knife for unlocking the door.

TAKING RISKS

Count Dooku may be eager to get away from the pirates—and the Jedi—but his clever escape plan makes him overconfident. Obi-Wan warns him that his escape route may not be safe, but Dooku likes to take risks. Unfortunately, he leads them straight into a gang of pirate guards—who are not pleased to see them.

TRUE OR FALSE?

The Jedi are captured after eating too much.

False: Their welcoming drinks are drugged.

WHY IS THE *MALEVOLENCE* THE DEADLIEST BATTLESHIP?

When it is first deployed, the *Malevolence* is shrouded in mystery. The ship appears as if from nowhere, destroys an entire Jedi fleet, then departs without leaving any clue to its identity. The terrifying truth is that it is a massive battleship with unprecedented firepower.

ION CANNON

The *Malevolence* contains the biggest ion cannon ever constructed. It can destroy the electrical systems of anything in its sight, leaving survivors helpless against Separatist trackers.

RUTHLESS GENERAL

The *Malevolence*'s commander is General Grievous and he revels in its power. With such an aggressive, blood-thirsty cyborg at the helm, the high-tech battleship becomes truly deadly.

FEAR FACTOR

Longer than four Republic cruisers put together, the *Malevolence* is larger than many engineers ever thought possible. Its size is a deliberate ploy by Count Dooku to make it the most feared craft in space.

SUBJUGATOR-CLASS HEAVY CRUISER

This dreadnought is an example of the latest Separatist technology. The ion cannons have an improved power supply, and advanced signal jamming systems help to mask the ship's location.

- **WEAPONS** 2 ION PULSE CANNONS, TURBOLASER BATTERIES, POINT-DEFENSE CANNONS, VULTURE DROIDS, *DROCH*-CLASS BOARDING SHIPS
- **LENGTH** 4,845 M (15,896 FT)
- **CREW** 900 DROIDS

COMMAND BRIDGE

TURBOLASERS AND LASER CANNONS

ELECTROMAGNETIC SHUNTS HOUSED IN SPOKES

WHY IS QUEEN KARINA'S ARMY SO

With countless diabolical plots to bolster his strength, Count Dooku has many armies to call on to break up the Republic and smash the Jedi. Some allies have the latest deadly droids, others develop fiendish weapons, but on the planet Geonosis skulks a truly nightmarish foe . . .

AN EVIL QUEEN

Thought to be a myth until discovered by the Jedi, Geonosian Queen Karina the Great can bring back the dead by animating their bodies with vile mind worms. Proud, power-mad Karina secretly schemes to send her battling bugs out across the galaxy.

SCARY?

TRUE OR FALSE?
All Geonosians are zombies.

False: Only Queen Karina's army returns from the dead.

IMMORTALITY

Their lifeless bodies controlled by one hive mind, Geonosian undead soldiers keep attacking even after having their limbs or heads sliced off. However, the Jedi later discover that these zombie enemies do have one weakness—bright light.

AN UNDEAD ARMY

Queen Karina's hidden army lies beneath the Progate Temple on Geonosis. Its foot soldiers shamble through the darkness of the tunnels, looking for living victims to snatch and convert into their growing undead army.

"MY EMPIRE IS FOREVER!"

QUEEN KARINA

27

WHY IS R3-S6 SUCH A DANGEROUS TRAITOR?

CAMERA EYE
RECORDS
SECRET
INFORMATION

A trusty astromech to serve the Republic—that's what R3-S6 was, until he became the target of a sinister plot. R3 was stolen just after his construction by agents of General Grievous, who changed his programming. He entered Anakin's service, but as the most disloyal droid in the galaxy.

EXTENDABLE
THIRD LEG
EXTRACTS HERE

He Betrays Anakin

On a mission into enemy space, R3-S6 sets off a tracking beacon that alerts General Grievous to Anakin's presence. When the Jedi tells R3 to "prep" the hyperspace engines, the droid lets them tumble into space instead, leaving Anakin an easy target for his foes.

He Attacks R2-D2

When the Jedi attack Grievous's spy base, R2 comes face-to-face with his rogue replacement! The treacherous R3-S6 tries to bump R2 off a ledge. When R3 finds that he himself is set to fall, he attaches a line to R2 to take him down too. R2 keeps his cool and cuts through the line, leaving R3 to fall to his destruction alone.

He Activates Enemy Droids

R3 shows his treachery when he accompanies Anakin onto a salvage ship to look for R2-D2 who is missing. The Jedi wants to snoop around unseen, but R3 switches on the lights and activates some assassin droids.

WHO IS R3-S6?

R3-S6 was built on the planet Nubia by Industrial Automaton. An R3-series astromech droid, this new unit has the R2-series styling, but features an improved computer brain, with a larger memory capacity to handle more data.

SWOOP-PILOT GOGGLES

COAT STOLEN FROM WROONIAN NOBLE

He Has A Code Of Honor

This freebooting scoundrel may be viewed by some as space scum, but Hondo does have his own code of honor. On Florrum, he stops his men from shooting Jedi Ahsoka Tano as she runs past. Unlike the Sith, Hondo can't stomach violence when there is no profit in it.

DOES HONDO OHNAKA WORK FOR THE SITH?

The galaxy is full of shadowy figures who refuse to play by the rules. But while pirates, bounty hunters, and assassins may be happy to break the law, it doesn't mean they are servants of the dark side. In fact, some outlaws make life very difficult for the Sith.

WHO IS HONDO?

Hondo Ohnaka is a Weequay from the planet Sriluur. A known kidnapper and spice-runner, he runs a large pirate gang based on the planet Florrum. Hondo fights well with an electrostaff, but avoids hand-to-hand combat if he can.

Unafraid Of The Sith

Surrounded by pirates after a crash-landing on Vanqor, Count Dooku tries to frighten them by telling them they are dealing with a Sith Lord. Hondo, the pirate chief, is unfazed. He knows that Dooku is outnumbered and takes him hostage to prove a point.

He Only Cares For Credits

Hondo has no loyalty to either side, just to whoever pays him the most. When he captures Count Dooku, he is just as happy to sell him to the Republic as he would be to sell a Jedi to the Separatists. Hondo offers Count Dooku to Chancellor Palpatine and Yoda for a cool million credits.

HOW DOES THE SOLAR SAILER SAVE DOOKU'S LIFE?

The *Solar Sailer* was a gift to Count Dooku from the Geonosians. He designed modifications that make it one of the most elusive vehicles in space. In times of great danger, the Count relies on it to escape and save his skin.

SOLAR SAILER

The *Solar Sailer* is 14.38 m (47.17 ft) long, but extends to over 100 m (328 ft) with the sail unfurled. Its interior is plushly decorated to fit with Dooku's opulent style.

- **MODEL** *PUNWORCCA 116*-CLASS INTERSTELLAR SLOOP
- **CREW** ONE PILOT DROID
- **MAX SPEED UNDER SAIL** 1,000 G
- **ENGINES** TWO GUIDE THRUSTERS, REPULSORLIFT ENGINE FOR BACKUP

FA-4 PILOT DROID GUIDING SLOOP

SHIP IS TYPICAL OF GEONOSIAN DESIGN

PRONGS ARE STUDDED WITH TRACTOR/ REPULSOR EMITTERS

HOLO DATA

The *Solar Sailer's* sail is made from a special material that expands when close to a star. It catches energy particles and uses them for power. This enables the ship to travel without using its engines, and so pass through space undetected.

STRONG DESIGN

The robust design of the ship keeps it in one piece when it crash-lands on the planet Vanqor. The ship's engines are damaged by Jedi fire, but its repulsorlift technology kicks in to guide it to safety, allowing its owner to flee his Jedi pursuers.

FORCE SENSITIVE

Brilliantly simple in design, the *Sailer* is perfect for those gifted in the Force. Count Dooku can make the craft respond to his thoughts, which is vital when trying to escape from the Jedi. He performs maneuvers with an air of complete calm.

QUICK GETAWAYS

Hunted by the Jedi, Dooku is forced to escape in the *Solar Sailer*. Luckily, the small, hard-to-detect ship is very quick to launch, aided by a single FA-4 pilot droid. Its guide thrusters give Dooku a good head start from his foes.

WHAT MAKES GENERAL GRIEVOUS THE MOST FEARED SITH ALLY?

HEAD ANTENNAE FO
COMMUNICATION
WITH DROIDS

ARMORPLAST
SHIELDING

Once a Kaleesh warrior, Grievous was rebuilt as a fearsome cyborg after a near-fatal injury. His savage delight in battle led Count Dooku to select him as the ideal commander to strike terror into his foes. Now, the Sith trust him to carry out their grimmest missions.

He Is A Cyborg

Born a scaly reptilian Kaleesh on the planet Kalee, Grievous was a famous warrior even before joining the Sith cause. Mechanical upgrades have made him terrifying in battle, with lightning reflexes and replaceable body parts.

WHO IS GRIEVOUS?

General Grievous is a master of military tactics, as well as hand-to-hand combat. His mechanical limbs have increased his height to 2.16 m (7.1 ft). Repulsorlift technology in his legs enables him to use them as extra hands.

He is Highly Skilled

Grievous is a master of the seven main lightsaber styles. He can outfight most Jedi, and delights in slaying them with the lightsabers of their fallen comrades. His four arms and unpredictable rotating wrists enable him to launch lightsabre attacks that very few Jedi can withstand.

He Follows Orders Without Question

A tactical computer, Grievous is the most trusted Separatist leader. If Count Dooku orders him to destroy a target, he does not stop to question the reasoning behind the command. This allows the Separatists to remain one step ahead of the Republic army.

Count Dooku has never before disobeyed an order from his Master, Darth Sidious. He knows that complete obedience is the Sith way. However, when Sidious orders him to destroy Asajj Ventress, he hesitates. Despite his cruel nature, Dooku speaks up for Ventress, saying she is his most trusted servant.

DOES COUNT DOOKU HAVE FAVORITES?

There is no room for friendship in the cold world of the Sith. Alliances are usually held firm by a shared belief in a greater cause. Count Dooku is typically stern and aloof, but he has shown a preference for certain followers. It is almost as if he likes them . . .

Savage Impression

Count Dooku is delighted and impressed by Savage Opress's monstrous physique. They first meet when Dooku turns to the Nightsisters for a powerful assassin. Dooku sees so much potential in Savage that he makes him his apprentice and even dreams of using him to take on Darth Sidious.

Grievous Ally

It is difficult to imagine anyone liking a murderous, rampaging cyborg with a hacking cough, but Dooku respects him as a formidable commander. When Grievous is captured by Gungans on Naboo, Dooku rushes to his aid and makes a deal to ensure the cyborg's safe return.

WHY IS NUTE GUNRAY SO USEFUL TO THE SITH?

The greedy viceroy of the Trade Federation delights in squeezing credits out of worlds that are too weak to defend themselves. His bullying tactics can lead to war, and that's just what the Sith want—chaos in the galaxy and a conflict that could destroy the Jedi.

ELABORATE VICEROY HEADDRESS

LONG FINGERS FOR COUNTING CREDITS

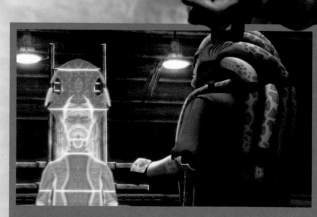

He Is Devious

Nute Gunray does not like to risk his own life in battle. He prefers to defeat his foes with sly tricks. The viceroy appears as a hologram to lure Jedi Master Kit Fisto into General Grievous's lair. Just as Fisto learns the truth, he is set upon by Grievous.

He Commands Vast Forces

The Trade Federation converts its merchant vessels into Separatist battleships during the Clone Wars. Among the most formidable are the *Lucrehulk*-class cargo freighters, which act as heavily armed droid control ships.

He Is Vengeful

Gunray never forgives a foe. Years ago, Padmé Amidala stood up to him and stopped the Trade Federation from invading Naboo. He is still looking for ways to get rid of her. He equally detests the Jedi, and will always support the Sith against them.

WHO IS GUNRAY?

Like all Neimoidians, Nute Gunray values wealth and possessions above all else. Sly and manipulative, he often tempts others into deals that they will come to regret. He fears his Sith allies as much as his Jedi foes, but has a slippery knack for escaping danger.

HOW IS DOOKU'S

A vast listening post for spying on the Republic, Dooku's Skytop Station is an immense battlesphere, under the command of General Grievous. Its sensors can pick up messages from all over the galaxy, and, most dangerously of all, spy on the Jedi Holonet. The station is giving the Sith an advantage in the war—a situation the Jedi want terminated.

INSIDE KNOWLEDGE

Skytop is equipped with more than adequate defenses, but there is one factor for which Grievous hasn't prepared. Astromech droid R3-S6 was spying for the Sith, but when the Jedi discover the truth, R3's inside data helps them to bring down Dooku's spy base.

HOLO DATA

Skytop Station's air defenses ordinarily consist of vulture droids and *Rogue*-class starfighters. General Grievous has bolstered its defenses with B2 battle droids and MagnaGuards.

SPY BASE DESTROYED?

STEALTH TACTICS

The spy base's massive sensor array is built to pick up long-range movements of enemy ships, but not individual intruders. By leaving their spacecraft behind and skydiving onto the station, the Jedi arrive undetected. Once aboard, the intruders place charges at key sites: the reactor and the engines.

SABOTAGE

When the Jedi's charges ignite, the Skytop's source of power is destroyed, leaving the spy base helpless. Its repulsorlift engines are blown to bits, so it can no longer defy gravity and remain in its location. In a blaze of fire and falling debris, the great spy station plummets to its destruction.

WHO ARE DOOKU'S DEADLIEST DROIDS?

To bring down the Republic and its clone army, the Sith need a mighty force of their own. As the war unfolds, Dooku relies more and more on droids. These merciless machines have no fear, never get tired, and never question orders.

Deadly Destroyers

There is no more sinister sight in battle than the arrival of destroyer droids, or "rollies." Their collapsible bodies curl up into balls as they speed to the scene of battle. Once there, they unfold, generate protective energy shields, and fire off twin blaster cannons that can devastate a clone platoon.

Sinister Supers

Super battle droids, or B2s, are heavyweights among droids. Larger and stronger than ordinary B1 battle droids, they are known for their hostile programming. They will even blow up droids on their own side if they get in the way of a good target.

Sticky Spiders

These sneaky-looking dwarf spider droids are hard to squash! They can climb any surface and their heavy blaster cannons are powerful enough to take out Republic ships. Spider droids also have a self-preserving feature—they reject orders that send them into areas of certain danger.

Good Losers

Deadly in their numbers, the B1 battle droids are the foot soldiers of the Separatist army. These simple, cheaply made droids are the unlucky ones who are sent into battle without cover to draw enemy fire away from the more expensive droids who do the important jobs. They are always eager to obey.

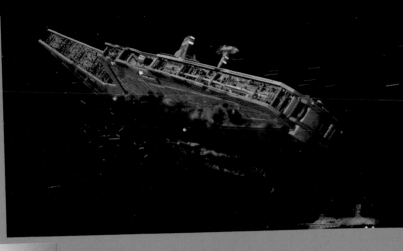

He Springs A Trap

At Ryloth, in order to conceal the full strength of his forces from the Jedi, Tuuk keeps four battlecruisers back in reserve. When the Jedi starfighters—led by Ahsoka—attack, Tuuk brings out his extra ships, surrounding and outnumbering his foe. The Jedi attack turns to retreat, with many fighters lost.

GOGGLES
LINK TO SHIP
SYSTEMS

SKIN CHANGES
COLOR UNDER
STRESS

WHAT MAKES MAR TUUK DOOKU'S SHREWDEST COMMANDER?

Mar Tuuk is a veteran Neimoidian captain and one of Count Dooku's most trusted naval officers. When put in charge of the blockade of Ryloth, this wily tactician rings the planet with battleships so that it is impossible for Republic forces to find a way through.

WHO IS MAR TUUK?

Mar Tuuk is from the planet Neimoidia. A cool-headed leader, he is in charge of the *Procurer*, a *Lucrehulk*-class battleship in the Separatist fleet. He is a keen student of military history.

He Studies His Foe

The first Jedi wave has been repelled, but Mar Tuuk does not relax. He calls up data on the Jedi ships and Anakin Skywalker, who is masterminding the attack. Learning that Anakin is a Jedi with unpredictable tactics, Tuuk orders his own ship to stay on alert.

He Saves His Skin

A captain knows his value to the fleet, and Mar Tuuk has no intention of going down with his ship. When Anakin pulls a surprise ramming maneuver on the *Procurer*, Tuuk instantly knows that his cause is lost. There are no last-ditch heroics for him—he leaves his droids in charge and makes a swift exit so that he lives to fight another day.

WHY IS ANAKIN SKYWALKER OF SPECIAL INTEREST TO THE SITH?

Anakin is one of the Sith's greatest enemies—a brilliant general who has smashed many of their armies and ruined their plans. Yet, the Sith have a fascination with this extraordinary young warrior. Will he cause their defeat, or is his path more uncertain? Whatever happens, they cannot afford to ignore him.

HOLO DATA

A prophecy says that, one day, someone will come to save the galaxy by bringing balance to the Force. Anakin's Master, Qui-Gon Jinn, came back from the dead to insist that Anakin is the Chosen One.

POWER STRUGGLE

Anakin has the highest level of Force energy ever measured, and Dooku is determined to prove his mastery over his young nemesis. Whenever Count Dooku battles Anakin, there is a personal element to the conflict. Dooku taunts the Jedi, constantly criticizing his lack of skill.

CHANGING LOYALTIES

Anakin has always been a loyal Jedi, but the Clone Wars have made him feel that following the peaceful Jedi code can be a drawback in war. As time goes by, his loyalty shifts to the Republic and the advice of its leader, Supreme Chancellor Palpatine. The Sith sense that he could be turned.

THE CHOSEN ONE

Jedi rumors say Anakin is the Chosen One—a special being whose powers will change the whole future of the galaxy. If this is so, how will it affect the future of the Sith? They need to be prepared! Even with all the battles and conspiracies of the Clone Wars to distract him, Darth Sidious keeps a special eye on Anakin.

THE

Many shadowy figures carry out the orders of the Sith: apprentices, bounty hunters, and even Republic traitors. But Ventress has been the most reliable. Count Dooku has called her his most trusted ally, and even Darth Sidious is afraid of her skill. There are many reason why Ventress is a Sith assassin like no other.

RUTHLESS IN BATTLE

Followers of the dark side are not held back by ideas of fair play. When dueling Luminara Unduli aboard the *Tranquility*, Ventress soon abandons swordplay and defeats her Jedi foe by burying her under an avalanche of metal pipes.

SMART TACTICS

Ventress knows that tactics can be more effective than fatal acts. Instead of taking revenge when she is shot at by Captain Rex, she uses the Force to control his mind and make him reveal the location of his Jedi generals.

GREATEST SITH ASSASSIN?

TRUE OR FALSE?
Ventress has had Jedi training.

True: She was trained by Jedi Ky Narec.

NATURAL SURVIVOR

A great assassin always lives to fight another day. When cornered on the Jedi cruiser *Tranquility*, Ventress leaps down a turbolift shaft, using her twin lightsabers to control her fall.

"NOW YOU FALL . . . AS ALL JEDI MUST!"

VENTRESS 49

DOES ANYONE LIKE COUNT DOOKU?

With his cold aspect and ruthless ways, Count Dooku is a figure of menace to everyone in the Republic. Yet there are others who like and respect him. Separatist supporters see him as a bold leader in search of peace, while bounty hunters enjoy rich rewards from his employment.

Hanging On His Word

As leader of the Separatist Senate, Dooku is a powerful and respected voice. The worlds that do not want to be ruled by the Republic have a parliament on the planet Raxus, where they discuss the Clone Wars with Dooku, whose words are highly valued.

Bounty Hunters

Life would be dull for these bounty hunters if there were no dirty deeds for them to do. Robonino relies on Dooku's schemes to keep him in work, and Chata Hyoki is happy to take enjoyable jobs from Dooku, like trying to assassinate Padmé Amidala. Dooku is a popular name with these low-lives.

Senator Bonteri

A long-time friend of Padmé Amidala, Mina Bonteri is an important member of the Separatist Senate. She admits to Amidala that she admires Count Dooku. Always careful to seem reasonable, Dooku pretends to want peace, which has fooled many like Mina.

Unlucky Lux

Lux Bonteri is a young Onderon who came to hate the Republic after his father was killed by clone troopers. To him, Dooku is a trusted leader who has the strength to stand up against the Republic. Soon, however, Lux will learn that Dooku is a dangerous man, when his mother, Mina, is killed by Sith assassins.

WHAT HAPPENS TO SITH

During the Clone Wars, the Sith like to encourage treacherous behavior to help their cause. A traitor may pass on information that will tip the balance of the war, or rise up and take action when the Republic least expect it. But treachery is a risky business and a traitor's reward from the Sith is often one that they do not expect . . .

SILENCED

Rish Loo is a Gungan minister who secretly works for Count Dooku. He tries to turn his people against the Republic. But when Loo is found out as a traitor, he becomes useless to Dooku. The Count ends their dealings with a thrust of his lightsaber.

TRAITORS?

SHOWN WHO IS BOSS

Faro Argyus is a captain in the Republic's Senate Guard. It is his job to watch over a valuable prisoner, but Count Dooku bribes him to help the prisoner escape. When his treacherous mission is complete, Argyus becomes boastful about its success—to the annoyance of Asajj Ventress. The Sith assassin stabs him in the back and takes the credit for herself.

TRUE OR FALSE?

Being a traitor is a good job with great prospects.

False! Traitors usually meet a grim fate.

REPUBLIC REWARD

The Republic also has to deal with traitors. Bitter clone trooper Sergeant Slick grew tired of taking orders and began passing secrets to Asajj Ventress. When his treachery was discovered, he was brought to justice by fellow clone trooper Captain Rex. The Republic treated him more kindly than his Sith allies would have—a long stay in prison is his reward.

He Takes Down Jedi

Using gadgets, Bane can match most Jedi abilities. His boots contain mini jet-thrusters to mimic Force leaps, and his stunners fell foes with energy like Force lightning. But if he can beat a Jedi, what could he do to a Sith?

TRADEMARK
WIDE-BRIMMED
HAT

WRIST-COM LINKS
BANE TO HIS
SPEEDER BIKE

LL-30
"PERSUADER"
BLASTER

CAN THE SITH REALLY TRUST CAD BANE?

Cad Bane is one of the most notorious bounty hunters. The Sith pay his outrageous fees because he is a proven Jedi-catcher whose underworld connections reach into places even they can't get to. But can such a sly character be trusted by anyone?

He Has Contacts

Bane's contacts help him get a lot of work and pull off many risky heists. When hired to steal a Jedi Holocron, he calls in a favor from shapeshifter Cato Parasitti, who impersonates a Jedi to pass through security. But Bane's many contacts could also be used against the Sith.

WHO IS CAD BANE?

Bane is a bounty hunter from the planet Duro. An expert shot with his twin "Persuader" blasters, he has no loyalties and will change sides halfway through a job if the other side is paying more. A knowledge of many languages, including Huttese, has helped Bane to make many contacts in the galactic underworld.

TRUE OR FALSE?
Cad Bane is a droid.

False: He is mortal but uses cybernetic breathing tubes.

He Is An Escape Artist

Bane is the master of daring escapes. Should he ever cross the Sith, they have little hope of making him stick around to face his punishment. When he is imprisoned on Coruscant alongside fellow bounty hunter Rako Hardeen, he stages a riot with the help of Boba Fett, and makes a getaway through the jail's morgue disguised as a corpse.

WHY DOES SIDIOUS ORDER THE DEATH OF VENTRESS?

The galaxy is in flames, Jedi forces are stretched to their limit, and Sith influence is reaching further than ever before. Yet, at the height of the conflict, Darth Sidious orders the death of one of his most powerful warriors—Asajj Ventress.

● ● ●

TRUE OR FALSE?
Sidious thinks Ventress is a wimp.

False: He fears her strength.

STRONG BOND

There has always been a powerful bond between Dooku and Ventress. She sought a strong figure to guide her and he saw in her the rare power and anger needed to create a great apprentice. Now Sidious thinks she has become too important to Dooku.

SIDIOUS DEMANDS LOYALTY

When Dooku speaks up for Ventress, saying she is his most trusted ally, Sidious becomes even more determined. Dooku is told that his allegiance must be to his leader alone. Ventress must be eliminated.

● ● ●

TOO POWERFUL

Ventress is told by Count Dooku that she has failed him for the last time. But she is actually guilty of too much success. Darth Sidious speaks to Dooku in a grim holocom appearance. Ventress's power is growing stronger all the time—she is now a threat to Sidious himself.

● ● ●

Conflicting Plans

Proud and independent, the witches seek the dominance of their own kind, and wish to see their own dark arts rule the galaxy. The Nightsisters are willing to help Count Dooku, as long as his plans do not interfere with their own agendas.

DO THE NIGHTSISTERS SERVE THE SITH?

The Nightsisters of Dathomir seem to be perfect allies for the Sith. In many ways the two groups are alike—they use evil to achieve their desires, they collectively worship the dark side, and they both hate the Jedi. But when it comes to helping Count Dooku with his plans, the Nightsisters seem reluctant to submit completely to the Sith.

HOLO DATA

The Nightsisters were once a set of warring covens. Mother Talzin united the clans and brought them wealth by selling their skills, especially in creating assassins, to the highest bidder.

Siding With Ventress

The Nightsisters are fiercely loyal to their own kind. When they discover that Count Dooku is part of a plot to end Asajj Ventress's life, the Nightsisters decide to go against the Sith to protect their former member. They secretly conceal Ventress in order to keep her from harm.

Plot Against Dooku

The Nightsisters have an uneasy relationship with the Sith—they won't be pushed too far. When they fall out with Count Dooku, the old crone, Daka, uses resurrection magic against him and his cyborg warrior General Grievous. Daka recites an ancient spell to raise a zombie army made of undead Nightsisters. This nightmarish force will follow only her commands, which are to attack Dooku's forces.

CAN ANYONE
DESTROY

Count Dooku has to do battle with more than just Jedi. He also faces the wrath of his own cohorts: Asajj Ventress, Savage Opress, and Mother Talzin. But even they may struggle to bring down the Sith Lord . . .

INVISIBLE THREAT

Enraged after Dooku orders her death, Ventress becomes invisible to wreak revenge on her former mentor. Cloaked in invisibility spells, Ventress and two other assassins try to slay him with lightsabers, but Dooku fights back by using the Force to sense their presence.

"KILL HIM, YOU FOOL!"

ASAJJ VENTRESS

COUNT DOOKU?

SAVAGE FAILURE

Dooku has trained Savage Opress himself, using his own secret methods to unlock the assassin's Force powers. When he is unexpectedly turned upon by this nightmare of his own creation, Dooku uses everything he has to fight back and escape.

TRUE OR FALSE?

Dooku cannot be bested in a lightsaber duel.

False: Opress disarms him but is bested by Force lightning.

EVIL UNDOING

When Dooku's forces attack the planet Dathomir, Mother Talzin of the Nightsisters retaliates. Using a lock of his hair, she creates a voodoo doll and strikes him down with a plague. Dooku is saved only by Grievous, who destroys the source of the magic.

WHY IS THE DEFOLIATOR DOOKU'S DEADLIEST WEAPON?

The Defoliator was created by Count Dooku's scientists for conquering enemy territories. The cruel device kills organic life, while leaving droids unharmed. It is a lethal artillery weapon that sits on top of a modified assault tank, the Defoliator Deployment Tank (DDT).

PORTABILITY

The Defoliator is heavy and cumbersome, but the Defoliator Deployment Tank is well-armored, stable, and strong. It can transport the large missile almost anywhere, across very hostile terrain, until it is within visual range of its target.

FIRE!

The Defoliator uses incendiary missiles. When they hit the ground, they explode, sending a scorching wave of fire toward the enemy. These deadly flames travel fast, destroying all living matter in moments, but leaving machinery, like battle droids, completely intact.

DEFOLIATOR

The Defoliator was created by the Neimoidian General Lok Durd. The large adapted tank can carry two droids, a driver, and a gunner, as well as the deadly Defoliator weapon.

- **MODEL** ARMORED ASSAULT TANK
- **CLASS** REPULSORCRAFT
- **LENGTH** 12.53 M (41 FT)

LAUNCHES DEFOLIATOR CAPSULES

ADAPTED ASSAULT TANK

TRIED AND TESTED

Dooku experiments on innocent civilians to try out his new weapon. He tests it on a peaceful Lurmen colony on Maridun, but they are saved by Jedi deflector shields. Dooku learns from this, and next time, on Dathomir, catches his victims off guard.

HOW IS SAVAGE OPRESS CREATED?

FULL SET OF ZABRAK HORNS

No Sith warrior has caused more alarm among the Jedi than Savage Opress. Count Dooku's new apprentice is like a monster, ferociously slaying anyone in his way. Savage was not born with all the evil power he now possesses, but he was fated to do his job.

Ventress Finds Him

Seeking a warrior ruthless enough to serve her, Ventress selects a group of Zabraks from the clans of Dathomir, and pits them against herself in a series of brutal challenges. The weak are cast aside or slaughtered until only one remains—Savage Opress.

PIKE HAS A SPEAR AT ITS CENTER

The Nightsisters Transform Him

Opress is taken to the stronghold of the Nightsisters where they weave their sorcery around him to create a warrior of unnatural power. As darkness enters his mind, he gives his life over to the sisters.

WHO IS OPRESS?

Opress is a Zabrak from a fierce warrior clan on Dathomir. He is a brother of the great Sith warrior Darth Maul—a connection that promises great prowess in the Force. However, Opress grew up unaware of Maul's existence.

HOLO DATA

The Nightsisters' sorcery changes Opress in many ways. He increases in size, strength, and ferocity. He abandons his loyalty to his clan, loses all traces of compassion, and gains Force powers.

Dooku Trains Him

Opress is later handed over to Count Dooku as an apprentice and faces a grueling training regime. Set impossible goals and punished with agonizing Force lightning, he feels a bitter rage that gives him new strength—enough to levitate massive stone obelisks.

WHY IS OBI-WAN THE GREATEST SITH ENEMY?

The Sith may seem like an unstoppable force spreading darkness across the galaxy, but Obi-Wan Kenobi is a constant thorn in their side. This warrior, diplomat, and spy could be the only thing that stands between the Sith and eventual triumph.

UTILITY POUCHES STORE PERSONAL ITEMS

JEDI CREST

TRUE OR FALSE?
Obi-Wan destroyed Darth Maul.

False: Obi-Wan cut him in two, but he survived!

WHO IS OBI-WAN?
Wise, kind, and peace loving, Obi-Wan is one of the most successful generals of the Republic army. As a youngling, he studied under Yoda and, later, Qui-Gon Jinn. Master to Anakin Skywalker, he is a clever negotiator and a major figure for good in the Clone Wars.

Master Of Disguise

The Sith believe they are the masters of deception, but Obi-Wan tops their scheming when he fakes his own death and has his face transformed to look like that of his murderer. Even when he is forced to fight with some bounty hunters in this new guise, he does not give himself away by using his Jedi powers.

He Never Loses

Obi-Wan has a reputation as one of the most difficult Jedi to defeat. Ventress, who is also a great warrior, has lost many duels against him. If there is a chance Obi-Wan may be outmatched, he is wise enough to take an ally like Anakin with him as backup.

He Foils Every Plan

The Sith often have schemes within schemes—backup plans to give them victory if all else fails. That doesn't concern Obi-Wan. When Dooku tries to kidnap Chancellor Palpatine, Obi-Wan is there—disguised as Rako Hardeen—to rescue the Republic leader and win the final round.

Mean MagnaGuards

Count Dooku's personal protection are the mighty MagnaGuards—elite droids with the speed, agility, and combat brain to almost match a Jedi in a duel. They work as a team, wielding lightsaber-proof electrostaffs to wear down the toughest foes. Even Anakin Skywalker has tasted defeat at their hands.

WHO ARE DOOKU'S MOST TRUSTED DROIDS?

In all-out war, Count Dooku needs the sheer destructive power of his battle droids. But some situations require brains, not brute force. For these subtle problems, Dooku calls upon machines with very different qualities—the elite skills of his MagnaGuards, the shrewd minds of tactical droids, or the sneaky expertise of his commando droids.

HOLO DATA

MagnaGuards are manufactured by Holowan Mechanicals. They fight as a group, attacking their foes from all angles. Magnetic feet enable them to run along walls and perform extraordinary maneuvers.

Straight-talking Tacticians

A tactical droid always tells it like it is! These droids' advanced software makes them highly intelligent. Wat Tambor pays the price for ignoring the advice of his tactical droid, TA-175, who tries to stop him from making a bad decision in battle. TA-175 escapes the scene of defeat with Dooku, but Tambor is left behind.

Cruel Commandos

These droids are programmed with special infiltration software that enables them to handle the unexpected, so they are Dooku's first choice for daring stealth raids and critical missions. Well-equipped as well as quick-witted, they carry E-5 blaster rifles and heat torches for burning their way into enemy strongholds.

WHY IS THE FANBLADE STARFIGHTER SO DEADLY?

The *Fanblade* is one of the most lethal starfighters ever created. The spacecraft swoops in like a bird of prey and inflicts hit after deadly hit with its laser cannons. In the hands of an ace pilot it is almost unbeatable. Unluckily for the Jedi, it is favored by Asajj Ventress . . .

FORCE POWER

The grace and strength of this craft work well with Force-sensitive pilots. Asajj Ventress uses the Force to become one with her ship, making the two of them even more formidable.

UNIQUE WINGS

The fanned wings on this fighter give it great speed and agility, enabling pilots to perform amazing, deadly maneuvers. They also act as a booster for the craft's deflector shield power, strengthening its ability to withstand attacks.

FIREPOWER

The *Fanblade* has the ability to pound its target with powerful laser cannons. Obi-Wan Kenobi experiences this firsthand when his fighter is pursued by Ventress. She finally forces him to crash-land.

FANBLADE STARFIGHTER

This unique ship is very rare, with only six of the craft in existence. They were created by the Geonosians for Count Dooku, and he gave one of them to Asajj Ventress.

- **MODEL** *GINIVEX*-CLASS STARFIGHTER
- **WEAPONS** LASER CANNONS
- **HYPERDRIVE** CLASS 1

PORTSIDE AIRSCOOP FOR THRUSTERS

CANNONS PIVOT WHEN SAIL IS FURLED

RETRACTABLE BOOM FOR SOLAR SAIL

SAIL MEMBRANE INCREASES DEFLECTOR-SHIELD STRENGTH

WHAT MAKES SAVAGE
THE

Even among the Sith, Savage Opress is a truly evil and cruel individual. Chosen as a servant by Ventress, given mystical strength by the Nightsisters, and trained as an apprentice by Count Dooku, Savage lives up to his name.

HE SLAYS HIS BROTHER

Opress is a loyal member of his tribe until Ventress and the Nightsisters discover him. Then the dark magic of their leader, Mother Talzin, wipes out his gentler emotions. Brutally transformed, he accuses his once-loved brother Feral of being weak and chokes him with one hand.

CRUELLEST SITH?

HE LOVES TO FIGHT

Many Sith slay with cool efficiency. Not Savage Opress! He enjoys bashing his foes, crushing them with raw power. Jedi Halsey and his Padawan Knox face Opress's full savagery on Devaron and neither survives to tell the tale.

HE GOES TOO FAR

Count Dooku tells Opress to bring him King Katuunko alive, expecting his orders to be followed precisely. But Opress will not risk the Toydarian king escaping. A powerful Force choke dooms Katuunko— and earns Savage the wrath of his Master.

DOES THE DEATH WATCH HELP THE SITH?

The Death Watch is a terror group from the planet Mandalore. Its aims are to restore the warrior spirit of the Mandalorian people and abandon peace. The group is proud and independent, but it seems to strike out against the Sith's enemies—almost as though they are working together . . .

Against The Jedi

Like the Sith, the Death Watch views the Jedi as the enemy and it fiercely opposes Republic interference in its planet. When Obi-Wan Kenobi arrives on Mandalore, the group's leader, Pre Vizsla, resolves to slay the Jedi. Despite these shared views, the Death Watch is wary of all outsiders, including the Sith.

Spreading Terror

The Death Watch and the Sith both use fear in order to gain control. The Death Watch begins an evil campaign of terrorizing the people of Mandalore to demonstrate how powerful it has become. The group plants a large bomb in the capital city, Keldabe. When it explodes, Obi-Wan Kenobi and Duchess Satine are close by and narrowly escape injury.

HOLO DATA

The Death Watch and the Sith are not allies, but they do share dark aims. The group proves its links to the dark side when it invades a village on the planet Carlac. Members attack villagers without remorse and shoot droids for sport.

Top Target

The Death Watch has singled out the peace-loving Duchess Satine of Mandalore for assassination. This is pleasing to Count Dooku, who despises the Duchess as much as the Death Watch do. The group almost succeeds in ending Satine's life when they plant deadly assassin probe droids on board her starship. Luckily, Obi-Wan is there to save the day.

NOT A PUPPET

The Son tries to lure Anakin to the dark side by leading him into anger. The Son casts a spell on Ahsoka, turning her evil. Anakin defends himself against her attack, but never tries to hurt her. He rises above the challenge and survives the test.

HOLO DATA

Anakin is vulnerable to the dark side because of his strong feelings and inability to let go of them. He still feels great pain over the death of his mother, whose life he failed to save many years ago.

DOES THE DARK SIDE ANAKIN ON

In a remote star system lies a world created from the Force itself. The planet Mortis is a magnet for those who are strong with the Force. Anakin finds himself summoned there by its ruling Force-wielders, one of whom, the Son, seeks to make Anakin join him on the dark side and rule the galaxy.

"YOU WILL BRING BALANCE TO THE FORCE."
THE FATHER

RESISTANCE

The Son offers Anakin an alliance, saying that, together, they would be unstoppable. But Anakin refuses to be tempted. He cannot turn away from all he believes in. In a final conflict, Anakin slays the Son with his lightsaber. The Father, ruler of the planet, dies in the battle.

OVERCOME MORTIS?

ENDING THE THREAT

Anakin refuses to fall to the dark side and rejects the chance to rule Mortis in place of the Father, who tells him he is the Chosen One. After the final battle and the Father's death, the Force-wielders' great temple on Mortis explodes, ending their rule. The threat from the Son is over and all returns to normal—for a while.

WHY DOES COUNT DOOKU FEAR PADMÉ AMIDALA?

The young senator for Naboo is a woman of strong beliefs. Secretly married to Anakin Skywalker, she desires a life far from the evils of war, but believes it is her duty to end the conflict that is harming so many. Unlike Count Dooku, she seeks no power for herself and puts her life in danger to help others. Her influence is not welcomed by the Sith.

SHE RESISTS THE DARK SIDE

Few can resist the pull of the dark side like Amidala can. She is even able to bring traitors back to the light. Senator Clovis, a Separatist spy, risks his life defying his evil masters to rescue Amidala.

SHE ALWAYS SURVIVES

Although she dislikes violence, Amidala is no stranger to action, and has survived many dangers. Even when Dooku sends bounty hunters Robonino and Chata Hyoki to destroy her, she manages to escape, this time in a daring speeder chase across the city. It seems she is destined to escape Dooku's wrath.

SHE CAN BRING PEACE

With a clear voice and a noble heart, Amidala can speak like no other on the importance of bringing peace to the galaxy. When she talks, all the worlds of the Senate listen. Peace would spell disaster for the Sith and put an end to their plans to gain power. Count Dooku begins to fear the speeches of Amidala more than the weapons of the Jedi.

HOLO DATA

The Sith think peace is a lie and that only through victory in battle can people become truly free. In a time of peace, the Sith could never perform the dark deeds needed to rid them of the Jedi.

COULD GENERAL KRELL BECOME A SITH?

A Jedi is merciful, peace-loving, and diplomatic—hardly a likely candidate for becoming a Sith apprentice. Yet, Jedi Pong Krell has certain characteristics which, when combined with his disappointment in the way the war is going, could open him up to the dangerous emotions of the dark side.

BLUE DOUBLE-BLADED LIGHTSABER

ONE OF FOUR POWERFUL ARMS

GREEN DOUBLE-BLADED LIGHTSABER

WHO IS PONG KRELL?

Pong Krell is a Besalisk from Ojom who was once a strict but respected Jedi general. However, he developed a fascination for the dark side to which he has now succumbed.

He Puts No Value On Life

A true Jedi will defend their clone troopers with their last breath. Pong Krell, however, does not think twice about leading his troops into danger that only a Jedi could survive. It is frighteningly similar to the harsh way the Sith treat their underlings.

He Revels In Destruction

The Jedi see war as a sad necessity, not something to be gloried in. Yet as Pong Krell gazes upon the destruction he has brought to the planet Umbara, a very Sith-like love of war burns in his eyes.

TRUE OR FALSE?
Krell is loved by his clone troopers.

False: He once was, but he loses all their respect.

He Uses Trickery

Typically, the Sith make sly plans built on trickery and lies. Krell shows how much the dark side has taken him over when he turns against his own clone troopers. He convinces his men that some of them are the enemy in disguise, and watches with contempt as they fight each other.

HOW DO THE SITH DESTROY THE

The Nightsisters of Dathomir inspire fear throughout the galaxy. Their sorcery can reach out and attack foes from afar, their assassins are highly trained and deadly, and their plots are far-reaching and devious. Yet, when they attempt to murder Count Dooku, the Sith waste no time in seeking their complete destruction.

RUTHLESS TACTICS

The Sith use defoliator tanks to scorch a path through the trees of the Nightsisters' stronghold, so the Sith forces can launch their ground assault with deadly speed. The spreading fires leave no shred of cover for the witches to escape blaster fire.

NIGHTSISTERS?

WITH DROID POWER

The Sith deploy their deadliest strike forces. B1 battle droids launch a direct frontal attack on the Nightsisters, while B2 super battle droids follow up with heavier firepower. Sneaky commando droids move through the smoke to strike down any survivors.

ASSASSINATION

Dooku knows that the true power of his foes lies with Mother Talzin, so he sends General Grievous to finish her off. Talzin escapes, but the general does destroy the clan's sorceress Daka, ending the supernatural power that controls her undead army.

WHAT IS THE

When Count Dooku decides to kidnap Chancellor Palpatine, he takes no chances. He wants only the best bounty hunters on the mission—and he chooses a grim way of selecting them. Evil scientist Moralo Eval creates the Box: a sinister cube containing a series of deadly challenges for the chosen mercenaries. Only the greatest will get out alive!

WATCHING THE DRAMA

Count Dooku doesn't just want to eliminate the weak, he wants to study the strong. From a control center outside the Box, he and Moralo Eval watch every triumph and disaster of those inside it. Dooku can talk to the contenders by way of a giant screen.

FACING DEATH

As job interviews go, this one is tough. The candidates must pass through a series of death zones, facing poisonous gas, robotic laser blades, and searing flame-throwers. The wise realize that even bounty hunters must work together to survive.

BOX?

ONLY THE BEST SURVIVE

Six unlucky victims fall to its terrible traps, lacking the killer instinct that the Sith demand. But the Box succeeds in its task—a final team is chosen. The remaining five will take part in a plan that will make its members legends throughout the underworld. Cad Bane, who rescues Rako Hardeen in the last test, is to lead.

"ENTER THE BOX— IF YOU HAVE THE COURAGE!"

MORALO EVAL

WHAT FATE IS WORSE THAN DEATH FOR A SITH?

NIGHTBROTHER-CLAN FACE TATTOOS

Ten years before the Clone Wars began, Darth Maul was defeated by Obi-Wan Kenobi on Naboo. The Jedi thought they were rid of him forever, and the Sith spoke of him as one now lost in legend. But Darth Maul did not die. He suffered an even worse fate . . .

Madness

Hiding out on the planet Lotho Minor, Maul is tortured by thoughts of his failure on Naboo and the terrible injuries he suffered. For years, bitter thoughts gnaw away at him until his rabid brain can think of only one thing—revenge.

LEGS REBUILT BY MOTHER TALZIN ON DATHOMIR

Depravity

Even a Sith must eat! To survive in a world of garbage, the once-haughty Maul has had to sacrifice his pride. He has made a vile bargain with a sneaky snake, who lures victims into Maul's ravenous clutches in return for his leftovers.

Junk World

Lotho Minor is the last place anyone would want to be, yet it has become the hideaway of this legendary Sith assassin. Used as a dump for all the broken bits of spaceships in the galaxy, it is toxic, vermin-infested, and stalked by monstrous fire-breathers.

HOLO DATA

Darth Maul lost his legs in his fight with Obi-Wan. Drawing from memories of his childhood, Maul used the powers of the dark side to construct a set of bizarre, spidery legs. They were later rebuilt by the Nightsisters of Dathomir.

WHO IS DARTH MAUL?

Darth Maul was a Zabrak born to the Nightbrother clan on Dathomir. As a baby, he was given to Darth Sidious to be trained in the dark side. Maul is obsessed with becoming unbeatable. His preferred weapon is the double-bladed lightsaber.

CAN A SITH DO A GOOD DEED?

Followers of the dark side can do surprising things at times, but one thing nobody would expect from a Sith-trained warrior is an act of kindness. Cast out from the order by Count Dooku and adrift on the planet Tatooine, Ventress discovers a side to her nature she didn't know existed.

SHE TAKES A JOB

Ventress joins a gang of bounty hunters hired to guard a chest on its journey by subtram through the planet Quartzite. As she and gang leader Boba Fett fight off raiders trying to steal the chest, everything seems to be going to plan.

SHE FREES A HOSTAGE

When Ventress finds a hostage inside the chest, she is shocked. Pluma Sodi is being taken to the tyrant Otua Blank and will be forced to marry him. Ventress does not want to see a woman torn from her family as she once was, so she decides to set Pluma free, turning against Fett.

SHE TRICKS A TYRANT

An excited Otua Blank receives his delivery and pays Ventress happily, but when he opens the chest, his bride is not inside. Instead, a bound, gagged, and furious Boba Fett is revealed!

HOLO DATA

Ventress is usually a lone ranger, but she needs money so agrees to join a gang of bounty hunters. Led by Boba Fett, the gang includes seasoned bounty hunters Bossk and Dengar, plus Latts Razzi and Highsinger.

COULD A JEDI AND A SITH EVER BE ALLIES?

Asajj Ventress and Obi-Wan Kenobi are locked on opposing sides. These two sworn enemies have a personal feud that goes back to the start of the Clone Wars. But Obi-Wan is a unique and unpredictable Jedi. And Ventress, although Sith-trained, never truly became one of their kind. Could this dueling duo ever end up on the same team?

WHEN SOMETHING CHANGES

Since being cast out by her Sith Master, Count Dooku, Ventress has learned to trust her own feelings. When Ventress discovers Obi-Wan has been injured by Sith warriors Darth Maul and Savage Opress, she is disappointed that someone has finally beaten her old foe.

TO BATTLE A COMMON ENEMY

Now Ventress is no longer working for Count Dooku, her former allies Maul and Savage have become her enemies. In fact, she came seeking the bounty on Opress's head. When she discovered that Obi-Wan had been ambushed by the evil pair, she decided to join the fight alongside the Jedi.

FOR SURVIVAL

Only by working together can Obi-Wan and Ventress outdo their two terrible foes. Ventress fends them off, while a revived Obi-Wan enters Opress's ship. The unlikely allies separate the cockpit from the rest of the freighter and fly to safety. Darth Maul and Savage Opress can only look on in anger.

GLOSSARY

ASSASSIN DROID
A droid designed to target and destroy specific people.

ASTROMECH DROID
A droid designed to repair and help navigate starships.

BATTLE DROID
A Separatist droid designed for combat.

BOUNTY HUNTER
Someone who is paid to capture or destroy wanted people.

CLONE TROOPERS
Republic soldiers who all share the same genes and look identical.

CONFEDERACY OF INDEPENDENT SYSTEMS
An alliance of planets and star systems that have declared themselves to be Separatists.

CREDITS
Metal coins or chips used as currency.

CYBORG
A being who is part robot and part living organism.

DARK SIDE
The evil side of the Force that feeds off negative emotions.

DESTROYER DROID
A battle droid that can shape itself into a ball.

DROID
A robot. Droids come in many shapes and sizes and perform a variety of duties.

ELECTROSTAFF
A long, lightsaber-resistant weapon.

THE FORCE
A mysterious energy that flows through the galaxy and unites all living things.

FORCE CHOKE
The use of the Force to seize an opponent by the throat.

FORCE LEAP
A huge jump made by somebody using the Force to enhance their natural ability.

FORCE LIGHTNING
Lethal rays of blue energy used by the Sith as a weapon.

GRAND ARMY
A branch of the Republic army made up entirely of clone troopers.

HOLOCOM
A device that enables its user to appear to others as a hologram.

HOLOCRON
A crystal box in which large amounts of data can be stored.

HOLONET
A galaxy-wide communications network used by the Republic.
....

HYPERSPACE
A dimension in space where starships can travel at super-fast speeds.
....

ION CANNON
A weapon that fires ionized particles to disable equipment.
....

JEDI
A member of the Jedi Order. Jedi use the light side of the Force to promote peace and justice in the galaxy.
....

JEDI MASTER
An experienced and powerful Jedi who is training a Padawan.
....

LIGHT SIDE
The good side of the Force that brings peace and justice.
....

LIGHTSABER
A sword-like weapon with a blade of pure energy that is used by Jedi and Sith.
....

MAGNAGUARDS
Advanced battle droids used by General Grievous as bodyguards.
....

NIGHTSISTERS
An ancient clan of witches who use the Force in their dark magic.
....

PADAWAN
A Jedi apprentice who is being trained in the light side by a Jedi Master.
....

REPUBLIC
The democratic government that rules many planets in the galaxy.
....

REPULSORLIFT
Anti-gravity technology designed for lifting objects.
....

RULE OF TWO
The rule that there can only be two Sith at one time: a Master and an apprentice.
....

SENATE
The government of the Republic. It is made up of senators from Republic planets all over the galaxy.
....

SENATOR
Someone who acts as a representative for their planet in the Senate.
....

SEPARATISTS
Those who are opposed to the Republic.
....

SEPARATIST SENATE
The government of the Confederacy of Independent Systems. It is the Separatist equivalent of the Senate.
....

SITH
An ancient sect of Force-sensitives who seek to use the dark side of the Force to gain power.
....

SITH LORD
A Sith Master or a Sith Apprentice.
....

SITH APPRENTICE
A Sith who is being trained in the dark side of the Force by a Sith Master.
....

SITH MASTER
An experienced and powerful Sith who is training an apprentice.
....

SPIDER DROID
A small, round battle droid with many legs.
....

STARFIGHTER
A small, fast, highly maneuverable spacecraft designed for battle.
....

TACTICAL DROID
A highly intelligent droid designed to act as an advisor to the Separatists in battle.
....

TECHNO UNION
A collection of firms who produce droids, spacecraft, and arms to sell to the Separatists.
....

TRADE FEDERATION
An organization that controls most of the trade and commerce in the galaxy.
....

TURBOLIFT
An elevator powered by repulsorlift technology.
....

VULTURE DROID
A starfighter fitted with a droid brain and controlled via a computer on a separate craft.
....

INDEX